WORLD'S WORST GERMS

Anna Claybourne

www.raintreepublishers.co.uk
Visit our website to find out more information

To order:
☎ Phone 44 (0) 1865 888112
🖹 Send a fax to 44 (0) 1865 314091
💻 Visit the Raintree bookshop at **www.raintree**publishers.co.uk to browse
our catalogue and order online.

First published in Great Britain by Raintree, Halley Court, Jordan Hill, Oxford OX2 8EJ, part of Harcourt Education.
Raintree is a registered trademark of Harcourt Education Ltd.

© Harcourt Education Ltd 2006
First published in paperback in 2007
The moral right of the proprietor has been asserted.

Editorial: Lucy Thunder and Harriet Milles
Design: Michelle Lisseter, Carolyn Gibson and Bigtop
Illustrations: Darren Lingard
Picture Research: Melissa Allison and Debra Weatherley
Production: Camilla Crask

Originated by Dot Gradations Ltd
Printed and bound in Italy by Printer Trento srl

ISBN 1 844 21495 8 (hardback)
10 09 08 07 06
10 9 8 7 6 5 4 3 2 1

ISBN 1 844 43998 4 (paperback)
10 09 08 07
10 9 8 7 6 5 4 3 2 1

British Library Cataloguing in Publication Data
Claybourne, Anna
World's Worst Germs: Micro-organisms and disease
616.9 ' 041

A full catalogue record for this book is available from the British Library.

Acknowledgements
The publishers would like to thank the following for permission to reproduce photographs: Alamy/Gabe Palmer III p. 25; Alamy/Phototake Inc. p. 23; Corbis/CDC p. 11; Corbis Sygma/Lorpresse pp. 18–19; Photolibrary.com p. 9; Photos.com p. 26; Science Photo Library/BSIP,LA p. 27; Science Photo Library pp. 12–13 (Chris Bjornberg), 14–15 (CAMR/Barry Dowsett), 20–21 (Barry Dowsett), 7 top & bottom, 8–9, 18–19, 22–23, 29 mid (Eye of Science), 4–5 (Russell Knightly), 10–11, 29 top (Moredun Animal Health Ltd), 7 mid, 16–17, 24–25, 29 bottom (Alfred Pasieka), 21 (Phillipe Psaila), 15 (ZEPHYR); Science Photo Library/USA Library of Congress 16–17; Topfoto/The Image Works/Sean Sprague p. 13

Cover photograph of The AIDS virus, reproduced with permission of Science Photo Library/NIBSC

The publishers would like to thank Nancy Harris and Harold Pratt for their assistance in the preparation of this book.

Contents

Some words are printed in bold, **like this**. You can find out what they mean on page 30. You can also look in the box at the bottom of the page where they first appear.

Germ attack!

When you get ill, part of your body stops working the way it should. You are sick and have a **disease**. For example, if you have a stomach bug your stomach stops working properly. It cannot do its normal job of breaking down food. Instead it throws it back up.

Many diseases happen when **germs** get inside your body. Some germs cause diseases like stomach bugs and colds. Others are much more deadly. They are the WORLD'S WORST GERMS.

The killer germs in this book are really nasty. They cause diseases that kill millions of people every year. Luckily, we have ways of fighting germs. But first, we have to understand them.

*This is a **microscope** picture ▶ of one of the world's worst germs. It is the dreaded Black Death. In real life, the germ is much smaller than this.*

disease	illness or sickness
germ	tiny living thing that causes disease
microscope	machine that makes things look bigger

All about germs

Germs are **micro-organisms**, or tiny living things. Some micro-organisms are harmless. Some are even helpful. But others can be deadly.

Many germs survive by living inside other creatures. Germs **infect**, or invade, your body to find somewhere to live. Once a germ infects you, it will make copies of itself. Then there are even more germs inside you.

Germs can be found in many places. They can be in air, food, or on animals. Germs can enter the body when you:

- breathe air
- eat food
- get cuts on your skin
- get bitten by an animal.

bacterium	type of germ
infect	to get into the body and cause a disease
micro-organism	tiny living thing
protist	type of germ that is like a tiny animal
virus	very small type of germ

Types of germs

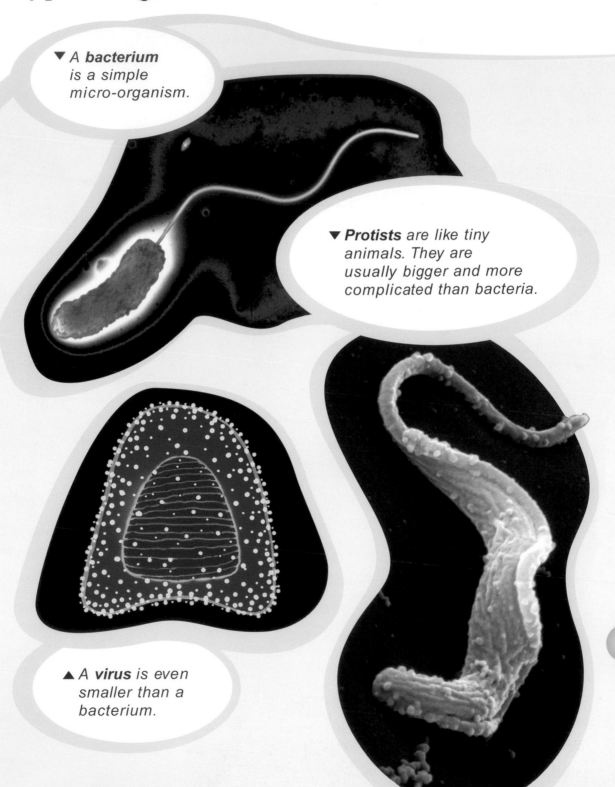

A **bacterium** is a simple micro-organism.

Protists are like tiny animals. They are usually bigger and more complicated than bacteria.

A **virus** is even smaller than a bacterium.

The Black Death

"Oh no, I've got the buboes!" Long ago, if you heard someone shouting that, there was only one thing to do – RUN! Buboes are swellings caused by the deadly Black Death.

The Black Death is a type of **germ** called a **bacterium**. Today, we can cure this **disease**. Long ago, most people died within days when they caught it. The Black Death germ got into people's bodies when they were bitten by rat fleas. Then people caught it from each other. Many people were sick and died

Black Death still exists today, but it is quite rare. Phew!

WANTED

The Black Death
(Also called: The plague, Bubonic plague)
- Last seen: Riding on fleas carried by the black rat.
- Crime: Stops lungs, liver, and blood from working properly.
- Protect yourself! Avoid rats and fleas.

▼ Rats often live near humans. Rats can carry fleas that carry diseases. Rat fleas jump on to people and bite them.

Malaria

Chills? Fever? Aching joints? Throwing up? These are the signs of malaria. This is a **disease** you can get from the bite of a **mosquito** that carries the **germ**.

The malaria germ is a **protist**. A protist is a germ like a very tiny animal. Once it enters your body, the germ **infects** your blood. Then your blood gets sticky, and cannot work properly.

Luckily, people can take medicine to keep them safe from malaria. Even if you get malaria, you can usually be treated – and live! But some people still die from malaria. It kills more than one million people a year.

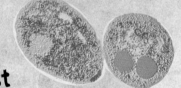

WANTED

Malaria protist
(Also called: Ague)

- Last seen: Hiding inside the malaria mosquito.
- Crime: Makes blood sticky.
- Protect yourself! Use **insect repellent** and mosquito nets to avoid mosquito bites.

insect repellent   smelly stuff that keeps insects away
mosquito   type of fly

Mosquitoes feed by sticking their mouth parts into your skin. Then they suck up your blood. If the mosquito is carrying malaria germs, these can get into your body. ▼

11

HIV/AIDS

Did you know your body has its own **germ**-fighting system? It is called the **immune system**. It kills most of the germs that try to get into your body.

AIDS is a **disease** that stops the immune system from working. That means if you get AIDS, you also get other diseases. Most people with AIDS die if they are not treated. But there are medicines that can help people to live longer.

WANTED

Human Immunodeficiency Virus (HIV)

- Last seen: In the blood and body fluids of infected people.
- Crime: Weakens the immune system.
- Protect yourself! Avoid contact with blood or other body fluids of infected people.

immune system	body system that fights germs
infected	containing disease germs

AIDS is short for **A**cquired **I**mmuno**D**eficiency **S**yndrome. "Immunodeficiency" means your immune system is damaged.

AIDS is caused by a **virus** called HIV. You can catch HIV from **infected** blood and other body fluids. Some people have caught HIV from dirty needles. The needles had already been used on someone with HIV.

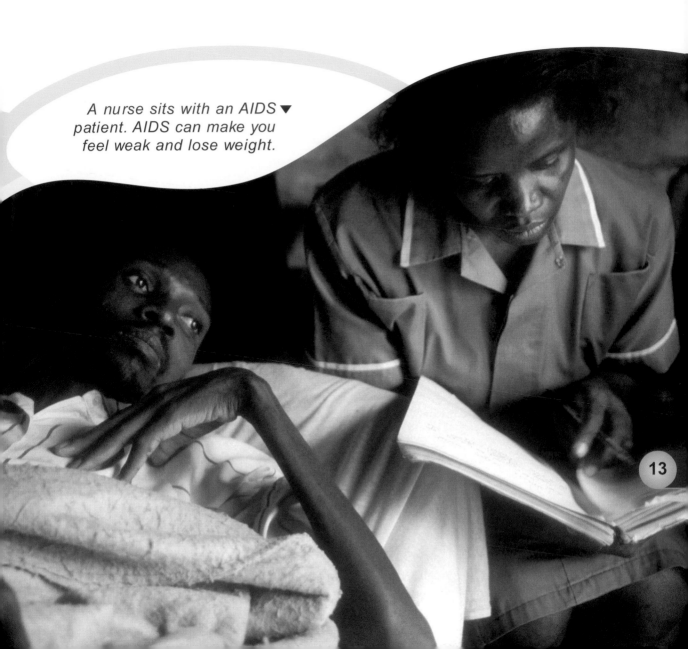

A nurse sits with an AIDS ▼ patient. AIDS can make you feel weak and lose weight.

Germ No. 4: TB

One in three people on planet Earth is **infected** with TB! The full name for TB is tuberculosis **bacterium**.

Most people's bodies can fight the TB bacterium. They do not get sick. But if you are already sick, TB can make you ill. If you have a poor diet, TB can get you! TB can be treated with medicine, but it still kills many people.

TB **germs** spread in the air through people's breath. When the TB germs get into your body, they increase in number many times. They eat away at your lungs or other body parts. They turn them into dead, rotten slime.

WANTED

Tuberculosis bacterium (TB)
(Also called: consumption)

- Last seen: Floating in the breath of infected people.
- Crime: Eats away at the lungs or other body parts.
- Protect yourself! Exercise and eat healthily to help your body fight TB germs.

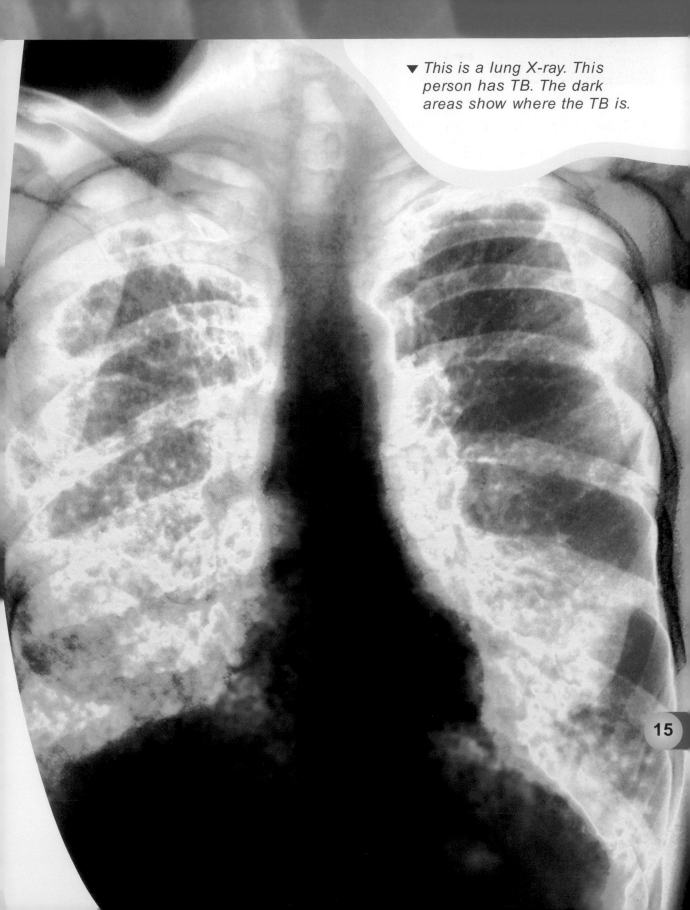

▼ *This is a lung X-ray. This person has TB. The dark areas show where the TB is.*

Germ No. 5: **Flu**

If you have ever had flu, you know it feels HORRIBLE. When you catch the flu **germ**, it makes you feel sick. You shiver, sweat, and hurt all over. But flu can get worse than that.

Flu germs spread through the air when people cough or sneeze. A few types of flu **virus** can kill older people. They can kill people who have a weak heart. Many elderly or ill people are given an injection to keep them safe from flu.

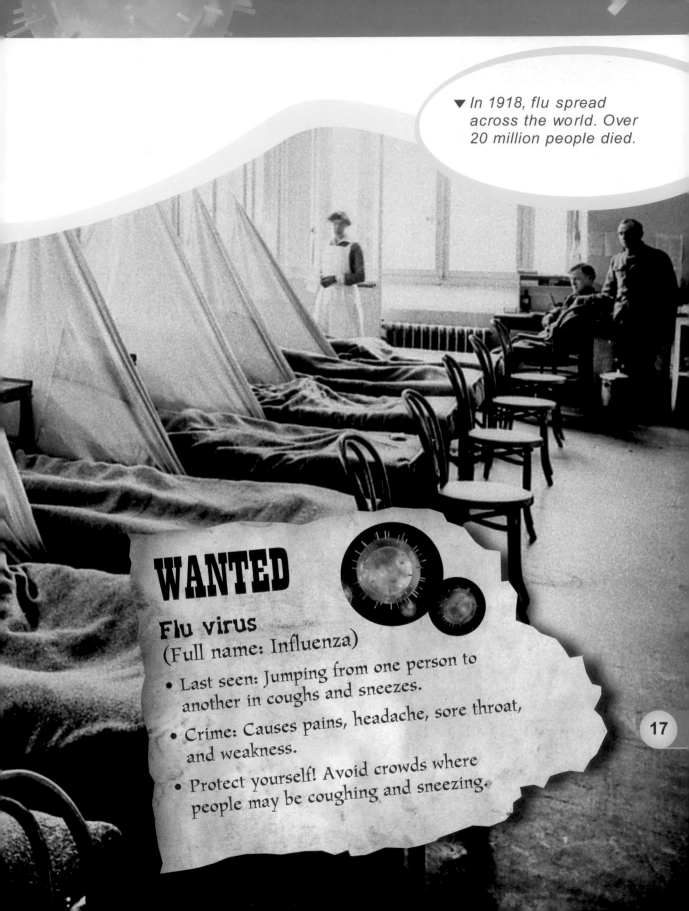

In 1918, flu spread across the world. Over 20 million people died.

WANTED

Flu virus
(Full name: Influenza)

- Last seen: Jumping from one person to another in coughs and sneezes.
- Crime: Causes pains, headache, sore throat, and weakness.
- Protect yourself! Avoid crowds where people may be coughing and sneezing.

Cholera

The cholera **bacterium** gets into your stomach in water or food. Then it makes you sick. You run to the toilet every five minutes. **Germs** come out of your body and flow away. Then they are ready to **infect** someone else.

Cholera spreads fast after floods and earthquakes. When buildings are damaged, waste from toilets leaks out. The germs get into drinking water and make people sick.

Cholera can kill in just a few hours if it is not treated. After a big disaster, it can be hard to get medicine to people. So cholera can kill lots of people.

WANTED

Cholera bacterium

- Last seen: Floating in dirty water.
- Crime: Makes the body lose water and get dried out.
- Protect yourself! Always try to drink water you know is clean.

▼ After a flood, finding clean water to drink can be a serious problem.

19

Germ No. 7: Ebola

Ebola has only been around for 30 years. Fewer than 2,000 people have died from it. But if you do get it, watch out! There is no known cure.

The Ebola **virus** can **infect** body parts, such as the heart or brain. It makes them bleed inside your body. In most cases, this causes death.

So far, only a few people have caught the **disease**. They have been mainly in Africa.

WANTED

Ebola virus

- Last seen: In the blood or body fluids of an infected person.
- Crime: Makes body parts bleed.
- Protect yourself! If there is a case of Ebola, stay away from the affected area.

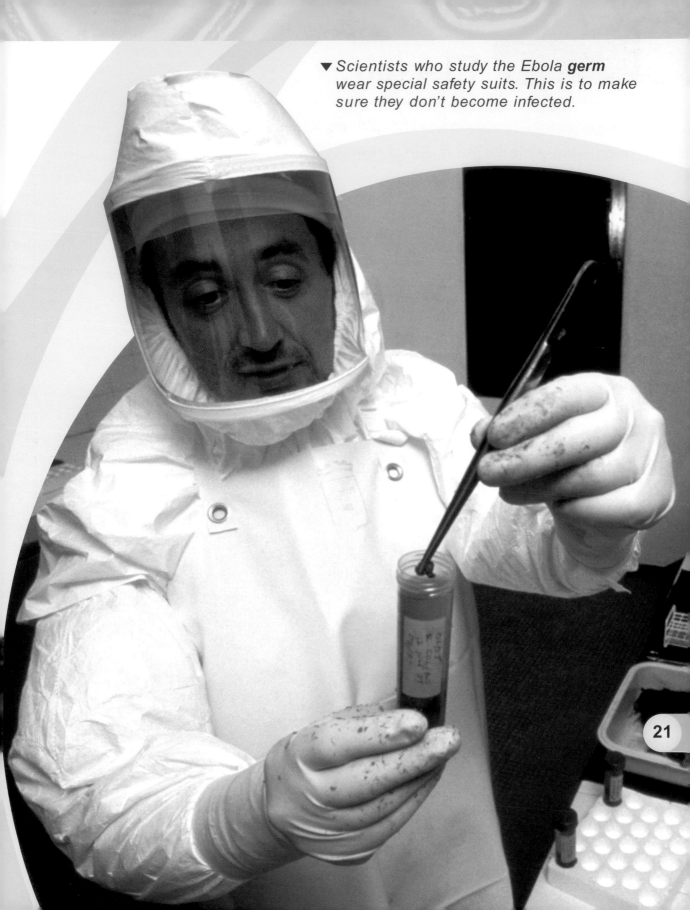

▼ Scientists who study the Ebola **germ** wear special safety suits. This is to make sure they don't become infected.

21

Sleeping sickness

Sleeping sickness is spread by the bites of **infected tsetse flies**. It is called sleeping sickness because it damages your brain. It stops you from sleeping properly.

Sleeping sickness can make you wide awake at night and sleepy during the day. You get a nasty headache, too. You need to take medicine to get better. If you don't, you may fall asleep and never wake up. Your brain is damaged forever.

WANTED

Sleeping sickness protist

- Last seen: Hiding inside tsetse flies.
- Crime: Damages the brain.
- Protect yourself! Use **insect repellent** to avoid tsetse fly bites.

tsetse fly   type of biting fly

▼ *In this picture, the tsetse fly is seen through a **microscope**. In real life, tseste flies are about 10 millimetres (0.4 inches) long.*

Rabies

Rabies **infects** animals like dogs, bats, and foxes. The **germ** infects the brain and makes animals go crazy. They might bite other animals or people. The **virus** gets passed on in the animal's saliva, or spit.

When humans get rabies they feel confused. They are scared of water.

If you have been bitten, you can take a medicine that stops you from getting rabies. Otherwise, you get the **disease**. Sadly, almost everyone who gets rabies dies within a week.

WANTED
Rabies virus
- Last seen: In many kinds of wild animals, including dogs and bats.
- Crime: Attacks the brain.
- Protect yourself! Stay away from wild animals. Report animal bites to a doctor straight away.

▼ People mainly catch rabies by being bitten by an animal that has the virus. Dogs can be very dangerous if they have rabies.

Stay safe!

It can be scary to think about all the **germs** out there. But don't worry – you can protect yourself!

There are many things humans can do to fight **diseases**. Our bodies kill most harmful **germs**. We also have medicines to treat most illnesses. However, for some illnesses we are still trying to find medicines.

The main reason germs kill so many people is lack of money. Poor countries cannot buy all the medicines they need. By helping poorer countries, the world could win the fight against killer germs.

Now you know about the world's worst germs. You are ready to fight them!

In some countries it is ▶ difficult to find clean water. You can stay safe by only drinking bottled water.

vaccine medicine that teaches your body to fight off a particular disease

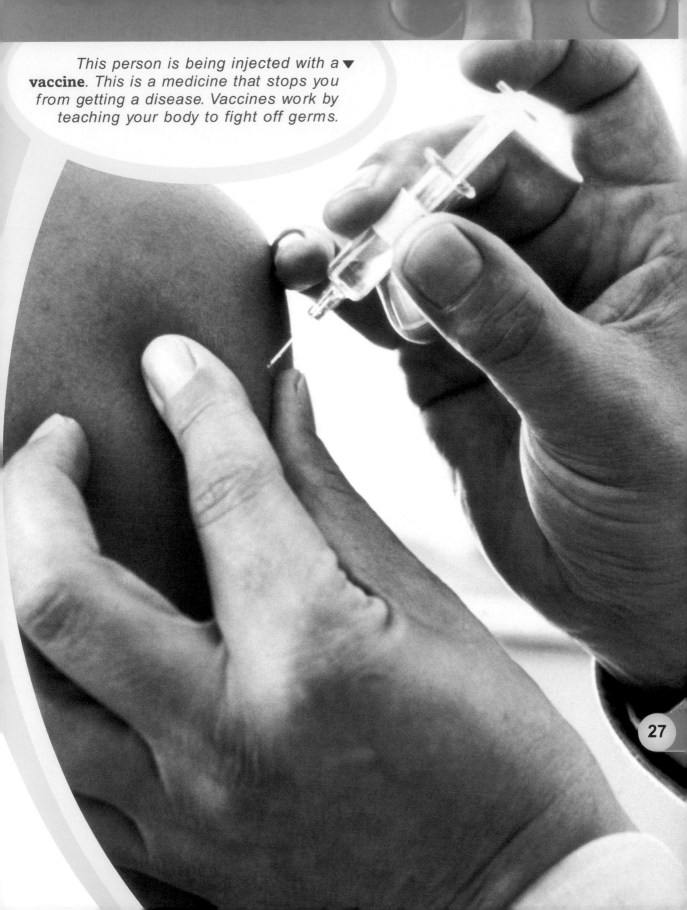

This person is being injected with a ▼ **vaccine**. This is a medicine that stops you from getting a disease. Vaccines work by teaching your body to fight off germs.

Know your germs!

Knowing about **germs** can help to keep you safe from catching them. Reading this book and remembering these important things could save you from a nasty **disease**!

Avoid becoming infected

◀ *Eating a healthy diet keeps your body fit for fighting germs.*

Keeping yourself ▶ *clean stops some germs from spreading.*

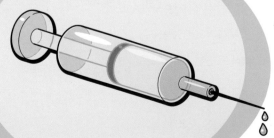

◀ *For some diseases, you can have a **vaccine**. This teaches your body to fight off germs.*

You can do other things to avoid certain diseases too...

Malaria

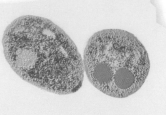

- Wear long clothes to stop **mosquitoes** biting.
- Use a mosquito net and **insect repellent**.
- In a malaria area, take special medicine to kill germs.

Cholera

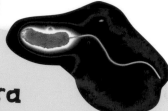

- Drink bottled water.
- Never swim in dirty water.

Rabies

- Stay away from wild animals.
- If you are bitten, go to the doctor straight away.

Know what to do if you become ill

There are medicines you can take that can treat many illnesses. A doctor will know what to give you. If you are sick, it is important to rest and drink lots of water. Then your body can work to fight off the germs.

Glossary

bacterium/bacteria type of germ. Bacteria cause TB and cholera.

disease illness or sickness

germ tiny living thing that causes disease. Many germs survive by living inside people.

immune system body system that fights germs. For example, tears are part of the immune system. They kill germs.

infect to get into the body and cause a disease. Germs can infect people through air or food and water.

infected containing disease germs. When someone has a disease we say they are infected.

insect repellent smelly stuff that keeps insects away. You might use insect repellent on holiday.

micro-organism tiny living thing. Germs are a type of micro-organism.

microscope machine that makes things look bigger. Scientists use microscopes to look at germs.

mosquito type of fly. Mosquitoes make a high, whining sound as they fly.

protist type of germ that is like a tiny animal. Protists cause malaria and sleeping sickness.

tsetse fly type of biting fly. Tsetse flies spread sleeping sickness.

vaccine medicine that teaches your body to fight off a particular disease. You can have a vaccine against many diseases, including TB and flu.

virus very small type of germ. Viruses cause flu, Ebola, and AIDS.

Want to know more?

There's a lot to know about Worst Germs! These are the best places to look:

Books to read

- *Horrible Science: Deadly Diseases,* by Nick Arnold (Scholastic, 2000)
- *A Serpent's Tooth,* by Robert Swindells (Puffin, 1990)
- *The Great Plague: The Diary of Alice Payton, London 1665–1666,* by Pamela Oldfield (Scholastic, 2004)
- *Infosearch: Microlife,* by Anna Claybourne (Heinemann Library, 2004)

Websites

- Ask Earl on the Yahooligans website to learn more about diseases and how they make you sick:
  http://yahooligans.yahoo.com/content/ask_earl
- Find out more about vaccines and how they can protect you from diseases on:
  www.kidshealth.org/kid/stay_healthy

Some micro-organisms are very useful.
To find out about them,
check out *Rotters!*

To see what your body parts can do when they are working well, read *Are You Tough Enough?*

Index